Barbie™
The New Song

studio fun BOOKS

White Plains, New York • Montréal, Québec • Bath, United Kingdom

Great news! Barbie and her band have been asked to play at the Homecoming dance.

"What do you think, girls? Are we up for it?" asks Barbie.

"Definitely!" answers Nikki.

"We rock!" says Teresa.

"We have to write a new song for the dance," says Barbie.

"Let's go to lunch and figure it out," says Nikki.

The girls jump into Barbie's pink car and head to their favorite cafe.

"We could write about the places we've been on tour," says Teresa. "Remember these photos from the yummy picnic in Paris, that amazing beach in Hawaii...and remember that fair in California?"

But besides that, they're stumped. Oh, no...writer's block!

"I've got it," says Barbie. "It's not so much where we've been, but that we've been there together! That's what the song should be about—it doesn't matter where you go, as long as you're with your friends."

Nikki and Teresa agree and the song practically writes itself!

*"No matter where we are
if it's near or far...
As long as it's we three
that's how it should be."*

The crowd loves the new song. It's a hit—
this is the best Homecoming dance ever!

How to Write a Song

There's no right or wrong way to write a song—just enjoy it and have fun!

1

What do you want to write about? A day at the beach? A boy you like? A fun memory with friends? List different things that are important to you and choose something you are passionate about.

2

Once you choose your subject, start thinking of words that go with your theme. Let your mind go! For example, if you want to write about a great party you threw, your list might look like this:

Music	Dancing
Balloons	Games
Friends	Party

3

Once you have a list of words you want to use, start thinking about how to put them into a song. Here's an example:

The music was great
We danced all night
My friends were there
Everything was right

4

Decide on a title. This can be the lyric that everyone will remember. Action words, images, and short phrases make good titles. Let the title be the message of your song.

Rock-Star Style

Accessorize with lots of glittery jewelry and belts, and don't forget a fun jacket!

Apply glitter to your hair, face, and body so you will sparkle all over!

Create some fun dance moves that you can rock to with your song!

Carry yourself with confidence!

How to Be a Better Singer

Follow these tips to be a singing sensation:

Pick a song that matches your ability. If you can't hit high notes, stick with notes that are lower.

Stand up straight! Good posture is the key to deep breathing so you can fill your lungs with the air you need.

Practice always makes perfect! Practice singing in the shower, in the car with the radio on, and even while you're taking your dog for a walk.

Breathe! Taking deep breaths will give you the most air to project your voice.